Everyone is Psychic!

An Introduction to Spiritualism

Terence N. Tompkins

January 2007

CONTENTS

CONTENTS

Author's Note

This book has been written to extend information to those on this Earth Plain, who are curious enough to explore the knowledge of healing and help that is available through psychic communication.

The startling fact is that there is a great deal that we can do for ourselves and others in a positive way, using our Spiritual capabilities alone.

This book has been written based on my experiences to achieve self awareness through Spiritualism.

Terry Tompkins

This book is dedicated to Kate, Keith & Lily.

ISBN 978-1-4303-1892-7

Chapter 1

Everyone is Psychic!

Everyone is psychic! This is a fact; a universal truth! Unfortunately many of us in this world have no idea or understanding of the amazing psychic capabilities that we are all born with.

With that said, the purpose of this book is to inform any reader, that it is possible to truly gain full self awareness, through the development of their psychic abilities.

I have set out below the various stages, with explanations and examples of my experiences that have brought me to my present level of psychic understanding. I have still a great deal to learn, and this may take more than one lifetime or level of existence to achieve.

We have the capability to receive information, from beyond the normal range of our five senses. This type of reception is called psychic. Radios and televisions receive electromagnetic energy vibrations that are beyond our normal senses and convert them into a range of frequencies that we can see and hear physically. This means that without the discovery of this form of energy, we would never know that radio waves exist.

It was discovered many thousands of years ago that we have the psychic ability to tune our minds to receive vibrations from the Spirit realm, through meditation. In fact Sir Oliver Lodge, (the Lodge of Lodge Spark plugs), based his early radio research, perfecting the coherer, upon his capabilities of tuning in these spiritual energies.

It must be realized that everyone's journey through life and capabilities here are different. It is important that we should all strive for self empowerment and enlightenment and to try and turn from the materialistic dog eat dog world that we live in.

I am positive that there are few of us, who have not experienced some form of psychic connection, no matter what their beliefs, as sudden inspired thoughts, or coincidences.

There are those however, with blinkered minds, who will not attempt any communication of any psychic kind with Spirit.

Some are not confident enough in themselves to take their capabilities any further than the experiences they have had already.

People with this attitude would be wise to stick to their beliefs until the time comes time for them to realize what wonderful spiritual (i.e. psychic) energies are universally available.

For those who are already questioning the validity of the so called truths that our modern materialistic, hedonistic, society has bombarded us with, and have an open mind but have yet to progress in true understanding, please read on.

Chapter 2

The Physical World Around Us

Firstly, we have to consider the conditions that are around us, particularly in the western world.

Most of us have been brought up and educated only understanding the physical world, with restrictive confines of dogmas set by formal religions, together with misinformation from governments and corporations, for the pursuit of power and control over us. As a result we have, for the most part been blissfully unaware of what is going on within the corridors of power.

Most formal religions promote the idea that the clergy has the only authority to communicate directly with their particular God figure and then forward such information or misinformation as they see fit.

Anyone that bypasses these requirements, are usually told that they must be committing sacrilege, a device to keep people under control through fear of excommunication or that they would go to the devil.

This can be believed for only so long, so that the hold of religion is more and more losing its grip. This results in people becoming more materialistic and for some to understand the true spiritual nature of our existence.

Governments try to keep us in fear in other ways, in particular in fear of war and of a possible collapsing economy both national and personal. The latest fears induced are the fear of Global Terrorism and pandemics, i.e. fear of the unknown and the unpredictable.

Under these conditions, the most powerful governments, together with the corporations, are steadily increasing their grip on all the resources of the world, for financial gain, under the banner of Globalization. The more that this is understood the greater will be awareness of the requirement for change.

The creation of fear is used to divide us, because if we stand united, we would be much stronger spiritually and be able to overcome these negative controlling energies.

We are supposed to learn from history, but I get the impression that what was happening in Germany in the 1930's is beginning to happen again.

Fortunately, with the internet and modern communications, it can be seen more easily, but people still need to wake up and take note.

It has to be realized that early psychics, who became the priesthood, found that people became believers in psychic or non-psychic information that they dispensed.

They found that this gave them the opportunity to promote an agenda that could increase their influence and power.

Most people in political power, together with royalty, over the centuries have been and are members of secret societies and have supported secretive governments, some of which have used the power of dark psychic energies, to keep themselves in the position of domination.

Typical of these societies or governments were the Nazi's, and now the Skull and Bones club, the Masons and the Builderburge group. However, because of the information available on the internet, their activities are no longer as secret. The Masons work on the principle that the wolves rise to the top and the remaining sheep are blissfully unaware of the truth and continue to unwittingly project the facade that these organizations do good work.

By the Church maintaining that the clergy were the only people authorized to have spiritual communication with God, they have maintained control by persecuting anyone that stepped out of line with its dictates over the centuries.

It is estimated that 4,300,000 people were executed during the middle-ages, because of their spiritual and clairvoyant capabilities.

The Spanish Inquisition, which was in operation for 300 years, and similar organizations, also tried to stop scientific advances.

As recently as the 1940's, psychics were prosecuted in Britain for holding Spiritualist circles.

One of the well known psychics, who suffered at the hands of the Law, was Helen Duncan, who was imprisoned and eventually died as a result of the stress caused by the persecution.

At one circle, during World War two, she reunited deceased sailors from HMS Bahram with their relatives, but the official news of the sinking of this ship had been made top secret by the government, for the sake of public morale.

These types of messages that she gave, made the military intelligence service furious.

Later on she was arrested on a trumped up charge and imprisoned for nine months in 1944, to prevent any possible leakage regarding the invasion of Europe.

She was visited by Winston Churchill in prison, and he was appalled by what had happened to her and he promised to repeal the witchcraft act after the war.

Happily, Winston Churchill had the laws relating witchcraft and mediumship removed from the books, in the 1950's.

We also must remember that there are many people involved in religion and governments that are totally and sincerely convinced of the credibility of the organizations that they belong to, believing that they are doing their best for the world.

However there are those that are convinced that they have to change the world to the way they want it to be, for reasons of gaining absolute power, via the set up of the New World Order? (Remember the New Order in Europe?)

It is not for us to judge their actions, but we should help them realize, that they will eventually be held responsible for their actions when returning to the spirit realm.

It is my understanding that we have all gone through many incarnations, hopefully to be able to strive for a higher spiritual existence, so that eventually we do not have to go through another trial and reincarnation here again.

Fear is the greatest restriction of individual Psychic expansion. I suggest that if we all know that we are responsible for our actions, both good and bad, and make amends for our negative actions, can we then advance and understand the truth of the universe.

Chapter 3

Truth of the Universe Never Changes

We are indeed fortunate to live at a time, where the awareness of the truth of the universe is being realized by a continually increasing number of people. The start of this movement forward began with Swedenborg (an early Spiritualist), in the 18th century.

As Spiritualists, (i.e. those that we can communicate directly with spirit entities), we understand that Jesus, from the recorded work that he carried out during his lifetime, was perhaps, one of the greatest Spiritualists the world has ever known. Buddha must also be considered as another great spiritualist, with the Dali Lama being his latest incarnation.

The Christian religion, as we now know it, was created initially by St. Paul, after he saw an apparition that he believed to be Jesus. As a result of this apparition, St. Paul considered that God had given him the mission to create Christianity, for which he used the basis of the Saviour God.

To make this religion acceptable to the masses, he incorporated many aspects of mysticism borrowed from Mithraism, Egyptian and other then current religions and this is how Jesus became the Christ figure.

However a conflict arose between the followers of Jesus and St. Paul's version of Christianity. This caused such a problem, that Emperor Constantine set up a committee in Nicene, to create the Nicene Creed in 325 A.D. and so began Christianity in its myriad forms that we know it today.

The Christian religion was set up with little tolerance for any other form of religion, or tolerance between the various forms of Christianity. This intolerance has been the cause of most wars up until the present day.

Spiritualists understand that we all and everything around us is part of the energy of the whole universe. Therefore part of the Infinite Spirit is within us all, and we all have the psychic capability of tapping into the life energy of the whole universe. Psychic phenomenon is a true demonstration of the spiritual connection between everything in the universe

Chapter 4

Growth of Materialism

With the growth of scientific knowledge, a great many became materialists, particularly those living in Western Industrialized Protestant countries that have drawn away from the Church. In my experience, growing up in England in the society in which we lived, we only pay lip service to religion, attending church only for christenings, marriages, or funerals, this only undertaken to satisfy convention.

This occurred, as it appeared to most that the Christian Church had no believable validity in the modern world. Therefore many people in Western Society have become materialists, atheists or agnostics.

Fortunately those that have learnt positive lessons from adversity, together with open minds are more likely to become Spiritualists. Spiritualism is a philosophy rather than a religion. As it will be seen as we progress through this dialogue

Many have no conception of true Spirituality of the universe, until they experience some spiritual phenomenon that is significant enough to cause them to realize that there is more to the universe than meets the eye.

Many believe that after this existence there is nothing, but increasingly this is not the case, as more and more people are being exposed to the true reality of continued existence.

The media is having a positive effect in changing these attitudes to bring people closer to the truth. Television programmes in particular are increasingly carrying more documentaries detailing psychic experiences to the general public, so psychic awareness is certainly on the increase.

Chapter 5

Protection, Control and Gatekeepers

Protection should always be established before undertaking any work with Spirit; this can be simply done by asking for it!

When it is asked for, gatekeepers move into place to stop any undesirable or mischievous entities, from the lower levels of existence, taking over our spirit. These takeovers can lead to all sorts of very bad conditions, such as possession.

Formal religions discourage people from working directly with Spirit, but they do not explain why it might be not wise for anyone to undertake this. Also it is not explained that we should all ask for protection from lower order entities, (from the dark side). In most religions these entities are called the devil or devils.

It also would be prudent, when starting work with Spirit, to be sure it is done so in a protected environment, such as in a circle within a well established Spiritualist Church.

As progress is made, whether in smaller circles, or as individuals, we should always ask for protection and that only the highest and the best Spiritual energies are allowed to come through.

Even those of us that consider that they are already well protected, it is still absolutely essential to always ensure that we have protective coverage.

I have to emphasize again, that it should be understood that we must all be in control of our lives.

This is important when working with Spirit, that Spirit entities, this includes our guides and helpers, clearly know that we are in control and have asked for protection. Otherwise the mischievous and negative entities could run riot. After all we are responsible for what we do!

Now can be discussed some of the more usual psychic experiences most people have gut feelings and coincidence.

Chapter 6

Gut Feelings

The strong physical feeling in the solar plexus, a gut feeling, is the most fundamental psychic feeling that all of us experience, whether we accept our psychic ability or not. It hits at a point known as a Spiritual point, or Chakra.

This point is the most sensitive that we have, and the reaction that we feel is usually very fast, so that we take immediate action in response to it. I am sure that most of us that drive have had a feeling that someone else on the road is going to do something silly or dangerous, this most of the time keeps us safe and out of danger.

Gut feelings can be a positive experience, and I am sure that many people have had these, similar to an experience I had earlier in my life.

After about eight years as an apprentice and qualified machinist, I decided that it was time for me to move out of the machine shop, as I had always had the ambition to become a designer. So I took a day off and went to several companies that were advertising for draftsmen.

At the last company that I visited, in Sunbury, Middlesex, I was interviewed by the plant manager. He informed me that they needed a tool designer and he offered me the job on a 3 months trial, on the understanding, that if I was not any good, I would have to leave.

He suggested that I should not accept his offer straight away, but I should go home and think about it before I made my decision. I arrived home and had some lunch, but I found myself with an incredible gut feeling that I must take this job.

I went back in the plant that afternoon, and again saw the plant manager, and told him, that the job he offered was such an opportunity, that it would be unwise to miss it. I started work at the company the following week.

I have since spent the rest of my life involved in engineering and designing tooling.

Chapter 7

Coincidence, Really?

Coincidence is another phenomenon that most people accept as being somewhat strange but not unusual. Spiritualists consider that there is no such thing as a coincidence. This idea is based on the understanding, that all things in the universe are connected. We are all, as everything else in the universe, made up of the same basic fabric. This applies to both seen and unseen elements. Everything in the physical universe is made up from atoms, and therefore everything is in vibration.

Because of this interconnection, what each individual thinks vibrates out into the universe. It is these vibrations that are picked up others, causing them to take actions leading to apparent coincidences.

It is easy to understand, typically, that this is why we meet or have a phone call from someone that we have recently been thinking about.

There are other forms of apparent coincidences, one being the writing of the Origin of the Species, receiving the credit for this was of course Charles Darwin, who was first to publish. Alfred Russell Wallace also wrote regarding the subject at about the same time. Similarly, inventions also have been produced at almost the same, an example of which is the Telephone that resulted in Patent battles, which through careful dating of his documentation, was won by Alexander Graham Bell.

The following information is based on the experiences that I have had personally, or know of first hand.

Chapter 8

Ouija Boards

Firstly, I advised that Ouija boards should NOT be used as these are the only means of communication that will allow entry of undesirable entities to bypass our gatekeepers and so create havoc even when protection has been requested.

Following is an example of what problems that the Ouija device can cause, and what actions were required to remove the entities that were creating the problems noted.

A couple of years ago I visited a family, living in an apartment on Victoria Park just north of Eglington Ave. in Scarborough Ontario.

I discovered during this visit that those I was visiting were well acquainted with Spirit entities, as they had experienced entities in the form of black shadows wandering around their apartment at night. These entities were apparently not bothering them at the time.

The family consisted of a mother, brother, two daughters, a son in law, married to the eldest daughter, and a young grandson. Just over a year ago the eldest daughter gave birth to twins, one boy, one girl.

With the increase in the size of the family they all moved into a larger apartment further north off of Victoria Park.

About three months ago, July 06, I had a call from the mother informing me that the entities that must have moved with them were beginning to bother her youngest daughter. These entities were appearing as cold black shadows and that they were causing bruises to appear on her daughter.

The mother explained that they had called in a priest who said that he could feel a cold energy presence. The priest undertook a procedure to exorcise the negative entities, however this did not work.

I therefore paid them a visit, and I suggested that I could try to remove these entities. This they agreed could be worth a try. So I went upstairs the place where the problems were occurring and suggested to the entities, that I could not feel, that they should buzz off and leave the daughter alone as they had overstayed their welcome.

I called them a couple of weeks later and the problem was apparently resolved.

I asked the mother at the time if she had an Ouija Board in the house, she said she did. I strongly suggested that she get rid of it a quickly as possible as could be the source of the problem.

Just recently, October 06, I had another phone call from the mother saying that the entities had arrived back with a vengeance. At night they were bothering everyone in the household, with them appearing again as cold black shadows and also apparitions. They were sure this time that the entities were there to cause them harm, as her young daughter was receiving bruising again. They also had to take action to protect the young children, as they felt that these entities were a direct threat to them.

Fortunately they were not afraid of these entities, although worried, considering them as a real nuisance.

I asked the mother if she had got rid of the Ouija Board, she said that she had not as she was scared of what might happen if she did.

I told her that it was absolutely imperative that the Board be removed from the house as this was the cause of their problems.

Upon contacting two Spiritualist Ministers, I was informed that my advice was correct, but added that the board should be sprayed with rubbing alcohol and then dumped. It was also suggested that open bibles be placed around the house, with candles burning.

These actions have apparently did the trick as I have not heard any more problems to date.

So beware the Ouija Board.

Chapter 9

We Are What We Think

Because our thoughts are vibrating, radiating energy, that directly affects the energy of the universe; we can become what we think. As our thoughts about ourselves are picked up by spirit entities, our guides, who in turn, with usually helping energy, direct us towards our goals, which can cause us to be who we want to be.

I am sure that many people, particularly those who are positive thinkers, know how this has helped them with their lives.
However there are those who do not understand this. This lack of understanding can cause them problems. This is why positive thought is so important.

We have to remember that we all have been born into this present physical existence, being primarily influenced in our fundamental way of thinking by our parents. Those of us, who were fortunate enough to be brought up by very positive thinking and loving parents, usually have a head start in being positive.

However, we are all surrounded by negative influences from those around us whether within or without the family, from the media, from government and many other areas. This helps create a negative presence of mind within us, which we should not have. It sometimes takes a great deal to overcome this, some people do not have the knowledge to get over it at all and have a tough life.

For myself, my mother was a very positive thinker, this was a great help, as my father, who was overworked and constantly worried because of the war that was being waged during my early years, had a very negative attitude, and so having negative affect me. It took a long time for me to overcome this condition, but I did eventually upon realizing where some of my hang-ups had originated, and managed to change.

This revelation was a great leap forward for me.

For those unable to overcome the difficulties from the bombardment of negative energy, may require help to change their thinking so as reduce or remove the influences of negativity. As Spiritualists know the movement forward from a negative to a positive attitude is the responsibility of the individual.

One of the principles of the Spiritualist Church is that, "Progress is open to every human soul". This means that everyone has the opportunity to improve themselves spiritually by moving upwards to a more positive spiritual level.

We have seen many people come into Spiritualist Churches, who are having trouble, and who, in a relatively short period of time, have been shown the tools to overcome these difficulties and truly blossom to a higher level of consciousness.

These difficulties have been and can be removed or reduced with helpful clairvoyant messages from Spirit entities, passed on to them by mediums, together with the taking Spiritual Healings, (more of this later).

My mum always used to say, be careful what you wish for, it might come true".

In my experience she was quite right, as many thing that I have wished for have come true. Wishing is of course a way of thinking of what we either require, or would like to happen in our future, again what we think can and will come true.

It is important that we ask Spirit for what we need, as if we do not ask, we will not get. This is unfortunately overlooked by many.

These are just a few of things that demonstrate the power of our minds that we all can command.

We also have to remember that apparently negative things that happen to us in our lives can usually turn out to be very positive. We need to make mistakes to learn from and progress. Those that believe that negative experiences are going to drag them down will not learn positive lessons from their experiences, unless they are helped realise that these experiences can in fact be a strengthening lesson.

Chapter 10

Sceptics with Closed Minds

In this world, there are people, particularly materialists, who are very sceptical about everything relating to the Paranormal.

Also there are those whose religious belief causes them to consider that all communication with the other side can only be works of the devil, with only the priests or clerics having the authority from their supreme spiritual being to communicate.

Those who are sceptical with blinkered minds will almost never be able to accept the universe as it really is whilst on the Earth plain, but some of them at least have an inkling of survival of earthly death.

These people have such a mind set that they are unable to accept anything other than what they are told to believe, which is very unfortunate. But at least, religious sceptics have a belief that there is another existence, although they maybe somewhat misinformed of its true nature.

Those who believe only, that this life here is all there is, are in danger of going into a form of limbo, when their physical life here has ended.

There are many spirits that have remained in limbo, usually due to sudden death, without having the chance to realise that they have died. But not all is lost as those in limbo can be helped by psychics, to move upward to the light (the next level of existence), with a process known as a rescue. (More of this later)

Chapter 11

Sceptics with Open Minds

Fortunately there are sceptics with open minds and they are a great asset to the spiritualist philosophy. They work hard to be sure that they have balanced view of the subject, because their questioning brings forth the validity of the philosophy.

What follows is information regarding one of these open minded sceptics, who admits that he found proofs of survival and spiritual communication.

A book published on the internet, written by Victor Zammit, who calls himself an open minded sceptic and a former attorney at law, who set out to investigate and refute the evidence for survival after death.

He came to the indisputable conclusion that there is a great deal of evidence that taken as a whole, that absolutely proves the case for the afterlife. His book can be found on line at: - www.victorzammit.com/book. Victor Zammit's main web site has a wealth of very interesting information, well worth reading.

When starting upon the road to understanding and working with Spirit energies, the cautious and safest approach, should be with open minded scepticism, which in my view is the correct one to follow, as fools rush in where angels fear to tread.

Cautious open minded scepticism was the approach that I took, moving forward at a pace that was dictated by my ability to fully understand each step of the way. My progress was paced by my teacher Rev. Bauld of

Springdale Church. There were times when she challenged me to take a quantum step forward, when she knew that I was ready.

One of the more famous sceptics was Harry Houdini, who had heated discussions regarding Spirit, with Sir Arthur Conan Doyle, a well known spiritualist. I think that Harry was disappointed that he was not able to get messages from his mother. He actually wrote a couple of books to refute Spiritualists; Miracle Mongers and Their Methods in 1920 and then; A Magician Among the Spirits in 1924. These could be interesting reading.

Chapter 12

Precognition and Near Death Experience (N.D.E.)

Precognition, usually of a disaster, is a sudden thought that pops into our imagination to prevent ourselves, someone close or even unknown to us, from moving into a situation of great danger or having a serious problem. It can be like a very powerful thought that will require urgent attention.

My mother, my wife and I have had precognition, some examples of mother's precognition are as follows.

Before I was 19 years old, mum saved my life five times, the last three, under circumstances that have no rational explanation, apart from precognition.

The first of these three incidents occurred when I was returning home on a bus from a meeting of our Boy Scout troop. As the bus drew up to the stop where I was to get off, I saw mum, from inside the bus, on the opposite side of the road. When the bus came to halt, I jumped off and started to run around the back of the bus to run across the road. At this point mum could not see me but she shouted out STOP! Instinctively I did, and a car whizzed right past my nose. If I had continued running, I would have been knocked flat, and perhaps ended up elsewhere.

The second incident was when I could first afford to pay my way to attend the annual Farnborough Air Show, in September 1952. When I mentioned this pending visit to the air show, mother told me that there was no way that I could go, so the only way I was able to see the show was to watch it on television.

That afternoon we saw John Derry, flying a twin jet prototype D.H.110, diving the aircraft towards the spectators, intent on breaking the sound barrier. However a wing gave way and the aircraft broke up in the air, killing John Derry and his observer, with the engines and debris killing 28 and injuring 60, when it crashed into the spectators.

Those that were killed and injured were all situated on rising ground in the spectator enclosure, and I, being quite short at the time, would have positioned myself on that hill to get a good view of the show, this would have put me right in harms way!

The third and most significant event happened in November 1956.

The Thames valley at that time of year was always and still is prone to thick fog. In those days, more often than not, it was combined with a lethal mixture of sulphurous coal smoke. Through this and from smoking I caught a cold that went to my chest, I ignored it for quite a while, but then it got suddenly worse and I ended up very ill in bed. The illness was accompanied by a very severe chest pain.

My condition continued to get worse until one day, the pain suddenly disappeared and I found myself floating up towards a brilliant light, the feeling that accompanied this condition was wonderful, but impossible to describe.

This of course was a Near Death Experience, (an N.D.E.). As I was beginning to really enjoy this experience, my mum suddenly burst into the room and shouted at me! This brought me very quickly back into my body with a continuation of pain. My first reaction was to say to mum, "Why did you do that? I was quite happy were I was going."

From that day until she died she was not able to explain the reason for her action, but it sure brought me back. My thoughts upon return, was that this existence was not the end of life and a realization that I had been returned for a reason. It has taken quite a while before I began to discover what this reason was.

One of the significant conclusions that I have arrived at, was hell was here on Earth. Also, that I no longer had any fear of death, as I knew that there was something ahead beyond this existence. I also felt that I was protected and returned to help the people and the world in some way.

N.D.E.'s have been reported many times in the news and TV media, so there is no doubt that this phenomenon is wide spread, so that many have had a glimpse through the veil to their next existence.

Another example of precognition experienced, was in connection with my work. At one time, I was designing a mould for a long time customer, and the thought kept coming into my mind that I should not be doing this particular design. This feeling was right as it turned out that this customer did not pay me for the work when it was finished. He is no longer a customer!

My wife, Barbs, and I have attended a number of weddings over the years. At least six of them Barbs, came out with the comment that the couple would not remain married for long and every time she said this she was right on, the first only lasting a week!

These are just some examples, of what I call precognition from which we had received information ahead of time. These warnings, some in particular, were to show how well we all can be protected, by pre-warnings from Spirit.

Chapter 13

Taking Negative Action

Taking negative action, or using negative energy, will never promote a positive condition. It generally creates a worse negative situation. This is of no help to anyone.
It causes more problems for the person using negative action, rather than trying to correct the situation with positive energy. It is a trap that many people fall into. I myself fell into this pitfall. I thought at the time it was one of the things that I was returned to the Earth plain to do. It was after the event that I realised how wrong I was. To further explain this, I have laid out the story as follows:-

When starting to work at a company that produced containers, as a plant and engineering manager, it was my task, with the help of very capable general manager, to get the manufacturing operation running efficiently. In this task we were very successful. Unfortunately, however, the sales did not achieve the required level quickly enough for the owners, so the day came along when the operation was sold to a competitive manufacturer.

The day before the takeover was due to take place, we were addressed by the new incoming General Manager. He assured us that after the takeover, everybody's jobs would be safe.
However this did not turn out to be the case. As plant manager, he gave me instructions the following morning, for a specific number of employees were to be let go and it was my job to inform them. This of course was somewhat upsetting, but I had no option but to carry out these orders.

With this auspicious start, there was worse to follow.

The new G. M. considered that the fundamental principles of efficient productivity did not have any validity. This did not go down too well with me, as what he was saying was complete nonsense.

As top management attitudes will always filter down through organizations, our operation became chaotic at all levels, with most of the upper levels of employees not knowing half the time what their real duties were.

Actions were being taken, initiated by the G.M. that made no logical sense to me. Orders were being given to suppliers producing inferior products and a consultant was hired who was a former employee unexpectedly let go from our organization. This made me suspicious of the G.M.'s motivations.

During this period, the company had a management get-together. This event was also attended by a member of the board of directors, who suggested to me that the new G. M. would be the greatest benefit to the company, I just bit my tongue, at the same time still thinking that correcting this situation was the reason that I was returned to this Earth plain. I believed that it was my task to undermine the G. M.

Of course I was completely wrong in my way of tackling the problem as in doing so I did myself harm without causing any improvement. I found myself going to a restaurant every lunch time, for a couple of beers to ease the strain that I found myself under.

My wife, Barbs and the kids understood the pressure I was under, so that they were able to continue to create the calm atmosphere at home, this was a real godsend for me.

The situation eventually became so bad between the G. M. and me, that I was let go and given a significant financial compensation to leave and to keep my mouth shut.

I later realised that I would have been much farther ahead, by trying the opposite tack, in positively attempting to help the G. M. to do a better job. However, deep down I still do not think it would have worked.

The whole experience although very rough at the time gave me a greater determination to eventually achieve the dream that I had of working for myself. So this bad experience eventually caused a positive outcome for me.

This example shows that it is possible for all of us to learn from negative experiences and to realign our minds, to deflect all negativity from ourselves.

Negative energies that we send out and those negative messages we receive, block the spiritual point located at the base of our spine. The blockage of this point causes us to be in fear and prevents us understanding our true spiritual power. It is therefore essential that we help ourselves and help others through Spiritual healing removing these blockages, (again more of this subject later).

It also makes one aware that the thoughts and attitudes that we send out are usually reflected back to us.

My mum and Barb's mum always used to say that misery loves company. How true, so we have always told our kids, that if they felt down, to stay away from those in a similar condition.

Chapter 14

Dis-Ease and Disease

It is already a well established fact that a number of people suffer from psychosomatic illnesses that are induced by their negative frame of mind.

The dis-ease caused by anger is also a primary cause of disease.

Spiritual healing has been known to correct these conditions, but more of this later.

The following are examples of dis-ease.

About two years after I had departed from the company that was mentioned earlier, as I had expected, the G.M. was let go. A year or so after this he died from cancer. I speculate this was the result of anxiety caused by guilt from his negative actions.

There was fallout due to his activities when running the company. Two employees, one who was laid off, and another who became unemployed at the removal of the G.M., were unable to find new employment. As a consequence of this, the first returned to alcohol and both, due to depression committed suicide.

These above examples show how a person's dis-ease in regard to their attitude can cause physical and mental problems that can possibly end their lives prematurely on the earth plain.

Again these are examples of what we think can be what we become. The opposite example of dis-ease is the placebo effect, where people take sugar pills and a cure takes place. Again this is because of a change in their attitude of mind.

Chapter 15

Protection and Attunement with Spirit

The first prerequisite for all psychic activity is always, (as mentioned earlier), to ask for protection from the negative influence from lower order entities, with only the highest and best spiritual energies being allowed to come through for communication and healing.

Before any work commences to communicate with our clairvoyant or healing guides, attunement is required. Attunement means, that through meditation, one needs to adjust the frequency of one's brainwaves to receive the higher frequency transmissions from the spirit entities. This tuning can be felt through what is called the third eye. The third eye is a Spiritual point or chakra located in the centre of one's forehead. It takes practice for this tuned condition can be achieved.

This attunement can be attained, by meditation in a quiet place, with total relaxation draining all problems and thoughts, from oneself down through to our feet and into mother earth.

Help is available to learn how to meditate, through the use of pre-recorded tapes, whether of soothing music only, or one with a talk at the beginning of the tape by a qualified medium leading one on an imaginary journey, and then into music for about 15 minutes, after which the medium calls one back to the Earth plain.

A qualified medium is usually an ordained minister of a registered Spiritualist Church or a person that has received certification as a clairvoyant from the church.

I found that when I first started with these tapes, I began to see within my closed eyes, a myriad of moving colours, and shapes. This, to me, was an indication that I was beginning to be attuned with my spirit guides. When the attuned condition is attained, clairvoyant messages can begin to be received, or our healing guides are able to bring through healing energy. At this level of attunement, it now also possible to ask the guides questions, either to bring forward clairvoyance or healing.

My teacher was and still is Rev. Doreen Bauld of Springdale Church, who not only has been of great help to me, but also to very many others.

Chapter 16

Spiritual Healing

A large part of my work with Spirit is connected with healing most with compassion can perform this without realizing it.

Such examples are mothers who comfort their children when hurt or sick; those who work in the emergency rescue services; nurses, doctors and related care workers in the medical profession; those who put themselves out to help others in trouble, the people who help those underprivileged that need a helping hand, etc,, such as those that contributed towards Tsunami relief for those in South East Asia, trusting that whatever they send will get to the right place.

Whatever is done to help, no matter how small, increases the positive energy of the world. This energy is required more every day.

Self and Spiritual healing is possible, but there are those that are unaware that it can and it is being done. In developed countries, most people believe that to relieve their medical problems, seeking conventional medical help is the only option. There is no doubt that modern medicine has made great advances and should always be the first place to seek help when physical problems arise. This can, however, be like shutting the door after the horse has bolted. As it is well known that a number of medical conditions are initiated by stress or distress from many sources. This is particularly prevalent today, with the bombardment of created negative stress and from the modern pace of life. These conditions could be partly responsible for the hospital overcrowding and ever increasing costs of medical help.

The medical profession has proved by undertaking studies that have shown what we think can cause cures to take place. Indeed, some doctors are teaching their patients the self healing power of meditation and imagination.

Some religions undertake absent healing through prayer, if it is genuine it can help, but it can in the form, where it has become ritualized, not have the sincere effect that was originally intended. We are told by our spirit guides that ritual, due to habit without sincerity, has little validity in the Spirit realm.

As Spiritualists we understand that we all can act as a healing medium to bring healing energy through ourselves to those that are in need of as well as for ourselves. We need to understand that we all have our own healing guides to help us, and those we care for, but most are unaware that this kind of help is available.

It should be noted that if you do not ask, you will not get. We must therefore ask for help, and it will be forthcoming, again what we think is what can occur.

All spiritual healing can only work within natural laws of the universe, and we therefore have to remember that help from Spirit is always available within this framework.

Spiritual Healing works by rebalancing the body's spiritual points. This removes fear and unwarranted stress, so helping the body to cure itself.

With absent healing, we call upon our and the recipients healing guides to come forward with healing energy to flow through to those who need it.

In my experience I have found that distance over which healing is sent has no limit. The healing has beneficial effects, without sometimes the subject being aware that spirit has been asked for it on their behalf.

Absent group healing can be undertaken, by a group sitting in circle. The procedure is similar to individual healing, with the asking for protection, then with group meditation and request for help from healing guides.

Each person in the group, at an interval of 30 to 60 seconds, speaks the name of the person requiring the healing, for each to start healing. When this process is completed, the group together are sending amplified healing to the individual who requires the help.

This step-up process is used so that the individual requiring the help does not receive a sudden shock at the start of the flow of healing energy. A sudden withdrawal is avoided by having each individual in the circle say their name again in turn as they stop the sending of their individual healing, again to reduce shock.

This same form of healing is also very effective when the person requiring help is sitting in the centre of the circle.

The other form of healing is touch healing, in some churches called the laying on of hands. This originated in Shere, Surrey, England at the healing sanctuary of Harry Edwards, who was the worlds leading exponent of spiritual healing. His healing capabilities were remarkable, and his techniques have been passed on to others working in affiliated churches.

It was 1997 that I took a spiritual healing course at the church, as part of a group, given by the then Springdale Church President Janet Kerr.

We had six lectures that expanded our understanding, that as being part of the universe, we are all able to bring through healing power to those who require it, with the help of our healing guides

There is absolutely no doubt, that this form of healing, where we ask our healing guides to work with the sitters healing guides, is very powerful. Protection and permission to work with the sitter's guides is always asked for before the healing is undertaken. During the healing, the healer can feel the flow of energy, and feel the energy of the sitter's spiritual points.

We get very positive comments from those who have received healing. This confirms that the healers have been successful in bringing healing energy from Spirit through their Spirit to the Spirit of those who require it.

The balance of the spiritual points of our human frame is very important, and these very often put out of balance. This out of balance condition is usually caused by the negative energy within our spiritual energy.

Most readers, I am sure, as mentioned before, have gut feelings, that are warnings, that there is something wrong going on around them, or as confirmation of the actions that we take in your lives are correct or not. This gut feeling in the solar plexus, is the action of one of the most readily felt spiritual points.

Members and I, of this healing class received our healing certificates on the 6 December 1997.

About twenty new students attend classes each year to become qualified healers. These classes are part of an ongoing process at Springdale Church; and therefore there is a continual increase in the number of people becoming aware of the help we can receive from Spirit.

It has also been clinically proven that self healing takes place, with the practice of meditation. It has been found that blood cells live longer in people that practice it on a regular basis.

Chapter 17

Examples of Spiritual Healing

One evening I was by chance at a Thursday night service in Springdale Church. At the start of the hands on healing, I was directed by Rev. Bauld to act as a healer for a certain individual who had sat on one of the healing stools. I did as directed and proceeded to conduct the healing.

My first thought that as I started, was this chap was really in need of help, because of his laboured breathing. I noted this with spirit, and I carried on with the healing. I also sensed during the healing that the sitter needed a great deal of compassion.

The gentleman left the church as soon as he had had the healing.

A few days later I had a call from Rev. Bauld, and she asked is it would be okay for the guy that I had healed to call and thank me for the healing. She explained that he was terminally ill, something that I did not know during the actual healing process. I told Rev. that he could by all means call.

The next day I received his call of thanks. He was grateful, because the healing had helped to remove his fear and panic, so that he could now sleep at night. He had been unable to before, as he had been afraid of not waking up the next day. I explained to him that he should really thank spirit and the healing guides, as my part was only to act as a channel for the flow of healing.

Healers do not always know directly the results their work with the healing guides, but in the circle on a Thursday, after the healing, we do get positive information regarding the healing from some of the sitters. This builds up information of the help that was brought through from spirit.

I attended two churches on different occasions in the U.S. The first was in Austin, Texas, the First Spiritualist Church, at 4200 Ave. D. This was a wonderful church to visit, with a very similar atmosphere found at Springdale. It also had a teaching program similar to Springdale's. Its membership was increasing, in spite of being in the southern Bible belt. The only real difference was that the healings that were carried out without touch.

The second was in Hartford, Connecticut. This was the Church of The Infinite Spirit held, in of all places, a Masonic Hall. The first thing that I noticed after I had some trouble to find the place, that the attendance was quite small. However, the service started included a meditation, messages and then a healing. The healing again was different to Springdale; it was a touch healing only down only to the shoulders.

Up on the wall of this Temple was a design based on an inverted pentagram. As soon as I saw this I asked for protection from Spirit. (More of this later.)

Chapter 18

Divine Inspiration

I am sure that most people have had some form of inspiration during their lives and perhaps not understanding where it came from. I was certainly in this position for a long time, not understanding its true origin of some of my thoughts, until I began to work with Spirit in 1996.

Some examples of what I received were connected with my work. Such inspirational thoughts occurred usually when taking a bath, relaxing in the warm water.

I have since found out that I was actually meditating in a very spiritual medium, namely water.

Some of these thoughts were connected with methods of improving the efficiency of my work at a container moulding plant.

These improvements, which were long overdue, once in place, increased productivity of the manufacturing operation. This was achieved through improved communications, with everyone involved in the running of the operation being updated, every 24 hours, as to the productive efficiency of each department. Thus; a clear picture of the plant operation at all levels was known and decisions could be made to maintain the level of productivity required.

These kinds of thoughts have been coming through to me for most of my life. Other examples are thoughts that I would receive in regard to tool engineering, which were to help to resolve tricky problems and to correct details that I had missed or were wrong. These thoughts usually would come to me in the middle of the night, so that I was able to update my work the next morning.

There have been a number of notable personalities that certainly have had significant positive influence on the world, maybe through divine inspiration. Examples are Isambard Kingdom Brunel, Nicola Tesla, Sir William Crooke, Edison and Sir Arthur Conan Doyle to name but a few. I am sure that there are many more to come.

Chapter 19

Electronic Communication

Electronic communication operates using a range of natural magnetic frequencies, as everything in the universe is a form of vibration. It is easy to understand that Spirit would very easily be able to use these frequencies to communicate.

Sir William Crooke who was an investigator into electricity and early radio communication was a Spiritualist. He invented the radio vacuum tube, or valve as they are known in England.

This invention inspired Edison, who corresponded with Crooke, to invent the electric light bulb. Crooke also invented the circuit frequency tuning condenser; this was also inspired by his spiritual work, relating to tuning in ones mind to tune in with Spirit entities.

It has been stated that Edison, whose parents were Spiritualists, actually tried to produce a machine that would be able help people communicate with dead. Several of his employees had seen the prototype of this machine.

Edison had come through to a circle indicating that such a machine did once exist, but however did not work. Much of his life Edison was an agnostic, but still considered that there was a higher being or energy in the universe.

In his book, Victor Zammit gives several examples of evidence of communication though electronic devices. One such method has been found to occur by setting a tape recorder to record in a quiet place, that has been found to have recorded spirit messages in response to questions.

The internet search engine, Google, has at least 50,000 listings regarding electronic voice communication.

I have yet to try this form of communication and the only direct knowledge of E. V. P. is through my mother who kept seeing our late son Keith's face superimposed over the image of John Wayne in television programs.

It all makes sense, when we understand that all is vibration and these vibrations can be tuned electronically, as well as our minds to a level at which we can perceive communications from other levels of vibration and existence.

Chapter 20

Physical Phenomena

Physical phenomena is usually attributed Poltergeists.

Actually it is usually the result of physical communication from spirit entities. The results can be quite varied the most commonly reported activity of these entities is of moving objects, sometimes as quite destructive actions. The destructive actions are usually the result of activities performed by mischievous spirit energy. In these cases, some may have to be removed through some type of exorcism, i.e. someone with good self control telling them to go.
A number of these activities have been video taped or filmed. Some have been investigated and found to have been caused from some explainable activity. However, many actions cannot be explained in normal physical terms, these can only be actions originated by the manifestation of spiritual energy.

Following are some examples of this type of activity that have occurred within my experience or received from witnesses.

Most have occurred since our son's death from complications caused by AID's in February 1996. We have, from that time, had a number of physical manifestations occurring at our places of residence.

The first happened when were living in the Minden Ontario area, in the middle of no-where that we called the Blairhampton triangle.

We had some of his friends staying with us one weekend and on the Saturday evening we had a bonfire on the gravel driveway leading up to the garage. At 10.00 pm the fire was put out and about an hour later, everyone retired for the night.

Two of Keith's friends slept on camp cots on the upper floor of the garage that served as my office / guest room. One of his friends woke up at 1.00 am, and asked Keith for a sign to indicate that he was happy where he was. Next he saw a cloud of sparkling light up in the corner of the room. Then he said to Keith that it was okay but it was not good enough and said he wanted to see a really big sign. Then the room was then filled with light, apparently from the bonfire. He got up and went to the window and saw that the fire had flames about six feet high. His reaction was to say to Keith that he now did know that he was happy, but to please reduce the fire, before the forest was set alight. It went out immediately.

On another occasion, a brass cross that had laid on top of Keith's coffin at his funeral, that had been put upon the stone work of the main fire place in the lounge, that after sitting there for about 18 months it fell off. This happened at about 10 p.m., on May the 4th. Why did it fall?

Someone who was staying with us at the time said to my wife, "isn't that strange, that it should fall off after all this time?". My wife Barbs said, "No it isn't, Keith did that". As it happens, Keith was born in the early morning of May the 5th in Redruth, Cornwall, England. The cross had fallen off on his birthday. I think that he wanted us to remember, as if we could ever forget!

I was once involved in a conflict with my brother in England regarding our mother's house after her death. Mother had given me her house long before she passed on but did not inform my brother of this. My brother decided to sue for half its value, doing this without any legal claim. Needless to say, he eventually withdrew his claim. When this happened I asked mother for a sign if this outcome was what she wanted.

Usually, when I asked mother questions, the answers came in the form of a spirit light. In this instance the reply was somewhat different. A few days had gone by and I had yet to receive a sign, so I asked her again. The following night, when I was asleep and alone the house but for our dog, his barking woke me up. At first I did not hear anything unusual, so I did not bother to get up. But I then heard a rumble that ended with a bump, I half recognized the sound. It did not indicate that someone was breaking in, so I stayed were I was. Our dog eventually stopped barking and I went back to sleep.

The following morning, I went into the bathroom and I was surprised to see the shower door closed, which is something that I never do after a shower. The noise that I heard was the shower door closing! This was the sign that I had asked for. The shower doors have Lilies across the top; my mother's name is Lily.

On the following Thursday, a message given by Rev. Bauld, informed us that it was Keith that had closed the shower door on behalf of mum, as he was able to come through with sufficient energy to do so.

Another type of physical phenomena experienced in circle is table tapping with taps giving yes or no answers to questions. We also have experienced the table moving around on one leg. We have yet to experience full table levitation but it is not far off.

The above examples demonstrate that spirit entities have variable capabilities for communicating with us on the Earth Plain.

Chapter 21

Apparitions

Apparitions are physical manifestations of spirits, when they wish to make themselves known or wish to communicate by other methods than already described in this text. These entities appear, only to those that are sensitive enough to pick up the spirit vibrations at the right wave length. Some pick them up without the knowledge that they have the capability, hence the great surprise when it happens.

As noted above, spirits have variable capabilities of communication; including various energies to appear as apparitions, this is also why we see them in various forms.

The easiest and most usual form of an apparition and therefore the most reported is as spirit light. Others entities are only able to come through as a cloud of energy. These forms require the least amount of energy to be created; this is why mum used the spirit light method to answer most of my questions, however, with Keith; who is capable of creating phenomenon requiring more energy, was able to cause the shower door to close and the cross to fall.

The various energies that spirits use to create visible apparitions, account for the other diverse types that appear here. Some of them appear as small people in full form such as leprechauns in Ireland, or full sized entities either as outlines, misty forms of as apparently solid figures. Some of these entities may also have voice or are only a voice that can be heard. When they only come through as a voice this is called clairaudience, (noted later.)

Following is one of encounters that I have had with an apparition.

The complete story of the first encounter is regarding someone I shall call B. the general manager of a company near of Toronto. Some time after I first knew B., he called me and said that he had a difficult problem and needed to talk to me. He already knew that I was working with spirit from our previous meetings. So we arranged to get together the following day.

At our meeting, he told me that he originally became the general manager, to improve the company's performance, after he loaned the company some money, to prevent its bankruptcy.

Unfortunately, he seemed to be unable to properly communicate his ideas to the owner and son of what he considered was required to bring about a recovery.
He was of German birth and upbringing and his method therefore for giving the advice, was given in the Germanic manner, which had made it difficult to be accepted. This was very frustrating for him, as his suggestions seemed to fall on deaf ears, particularly as he needed to protect his assets in the company.

The situation got so bad, from trying to put his point across, he had been physically threatened, hence our meeting.

My advice to him was that the way he was presenting his ideas has to be all wrong, as what he was getting back was a reflected attitude of his approach. I suggested that he should, every time that he went into work from then on, imagine himself in a yellow balloon of protection, through which anything of a negative nature could not penetrate.

I also suggested that the basic motivation that he had for working at the company, which was one of help and healing, should be kept in mind while letting his inner light to shine out. With this attitude, I expected that he would see a fundamental turnaround in whole scenario.

About 4 weeks later I phoned him and asked how he was getting on. He informed me that upon the application of the ideas discussed, the change was like moving from night into day. He was so pleased that things were beginning to now work towards the direction that he had originally hoped.

However, another development took place.

About six months later, very early one Monday morning, I awoke to see a spiritual image before me, it looked as though it were B., I thought, "B, what are you doing here, you can't be dead".

At the time I did not hear any sound. Then I thought that if it could not be B., but was perhaps Alec Guinness. When I got up in the morning, I said to Barbs, "we should watch the news I think Alec Guinness is dead". However there was no such news. Barbs mentioned that she had heard voices in the night but could not quite make out what they were saying. The whole episode faded from my mind over the next couple of days, until Thursday.

On Thursday afternoon whilst I was at a customer's plant, I decided to call home in case there were any messages for me. As it happened there was one from the owner of B's company. It was too late to call at that time, so I decided to call the next morning. As I hung up the phone, it came to me that B. was dead.

The next morning I phoned the plant and asked to speak to the owner as I was returning his call. I was informed that he was not in at that time, so the receptionist asked, "Would you like to know what his call was about?"

"Yes, why don't you tell me?" I replied. "Well" she said "B. fell off a ladder at his home last Sunday, whilst working on the roof of his house, and was killed outright when he hit the ground. His funeral is this afternoon, and the owner thought you might like to attend." I did not go but realized that B. had already been to see me to say goodbye, in the form of an apparition.

I was later made aware that those whom have been helped sometimes come to visit to say thanks before going off to the next level of existence. These events usually take place within twenty-four hours of their passing.

Another apparition was experienced by my mother.

A short time before mother became ill and to eventually finish her days in a nursing home she had a visit from a spirit entity, a figure, wearing a black hooded monk's habit. I asked her was she frightened by this visit, she said no. She did ask me why this entity had shown up, my reply was that he was there to check and see how she was doing.

When consulting with our friend June, in England, I found that this visit was probably to ask mum if she would like to take a trip with him from which she could return if she wished. However, mum just said to him, ‘thanks for coming”, and he then duly departed. After this visit mum made her own funeral arrangements.

Mum did say when she was in the nursing home that she had a feeling that the entity came to see her to let her know that her time here was coming to an end.

Some people are fortunate enough to have the gift of healing and good communication with spirit from a very early age, hopefully these kids are no longer discouraged from communicating with there spirit friends, but are encouraged to continue to develop their abilities.

I had an interesting example of a young girl’s ability to do this, when I had lunch in Tim Horton’s one Saturday in Barrie. After passing two Tim Horton’s coffee shops, with the thought that I did not want to go into them, I went into the third Tim Horton’s that I came to. I sat down to eat my sandwich and a little girl on the next table started to talk, I thought to me. I said, “Excuse me, are you talking to me?” Her mother interjected saying that she was talking to her friend in the empty chair opposite me

My first reaction was to say how wonderful it was, and explained that I was a spiritualist.

I went on to explain that her daughter should not be discouraged in communicating with her friend if she was not afraid of the entity, of which she wasn’t. I mentioned to the mother that if anything from spirit did make her afraid she could tell it to go back to where it came from, as she should always be in control of her own life.

I also explained what I understood spiritualism to be, and some of the experiences that I had had.

All during our conversation the little girl nodded her head confirming all that I was discussing.

I am sure that I was guided to this particular coffee house so that I would be able to help the child's mother understand something of how Spiritualism works.

I asked the little girl to thank her friend for arranging for our meeting. It was also great confirmation of all that I had learnt about Spirit.

This also was a typical example of a Spirit entity tuned only to appear to a certain individual as the mother and I could not see the entity. It also clearly indicates how much more sensitive children are to such phenomena before they are adversely affected by the physical world around us.

Chapter 22

Pendulums

Pendulums are a very useful tool for communicating with Spirit. When one first obtains a pendulum, it should be worn by the person who is to use it for about a week; this allows it to absorb the vibratory energies of the wearer. Once this is done, there are a number of ways in which the device can be used to communicate with Spirit.

Some users hold the pendulum with one hand in space, then ask Spirit a question, to which the pendulum usually reacts in a particular swing or circle motion, peculiar to the person using it and interprets this movement.

I, because the single hand holding system is open to scepticism, place both of my elbows upon a firm surface and use two hands to hold the pendulum. This enables the support for the pendulum to be as steady as I can make it.

For a yes answer to my questions, my pendulum will swing back and forth, at about 45 degrees, for a no answer its swing movement will be at an angle of about 135 degrees.

It has been about 90% correct in its answers the remaining 10% may have been influenced by my wishful thinking.

Chapter 23

De-Materializations Re-Materializations

Materializations and dematerializations are the apparent appearance or disappearance of physical objects. This phenomena has been witnessed by many of us, and can be somewhat perplexing. Materializations have been demonstrated by eastern mystics for many centuries. It is a demonstration of an indication that the physical world is not what it appears to be to most of us, a solid immovable reality.

This form of activity goes a long way, to help understand what spiritualists have been saying for a long time, that this physical existence that we experience is not a true reality and that objects can transcend to other levels of existence. This has been supported by some of my experiences and by theories proposed by the study of quantum physics. The eastern mystics can cause these events to consciously occur, but those that I have experienced have occurred without any apparent rhyme or reason.

I have had a couple of de-materializations and re-materializations, the first being a disappearance of a vee block and after three months of search made a reappearance in my workshop.

The second was the disappearance of an old photo album that originally belonged to my mother-in –law. The disappearance occurred while Barbs and I were going through storage boxes of our photographs and we definitely had the album at that time and returned it to one of the storage boxes, however the same evening we went through the boxes for the album again but were unable to find it.

A few weeks later we moved house but we still did not find it, even after another search of the boxes and completely emptying out the house.

When we had moved into our new place, we were going through the boxes once again and found had returned album to one of them.

This is all possible if we realise that everything is vibration, and that physical objects and even people can be caused to vibrate at a frequency that we cannot physically perceive with our five senses.

This condition has been demonstrated with hypnosis, were a subject under this condition was told that he would not be able to see a person in front of him in a crowded room when he was woken, and sure enough he could not see his daughter. He was even able to see the time on a watch that was hidden behind his daughter. This event has been described in a book called “Holographic Universe”. The same kind of phenomena is described in a movie called “What The (Bleep) Do We Know”. The book and the film are based on quantum physics, (more later).

Chapter 24

Materialization

There is another form of materialization that I have yet to witness. This occurs when a medium in circle and in trance is able to produce from within their body a material called ectoplasm. This material is able to coalesce into a form of a person, usually known to at least one of the sitters. They usually communicate with voice. This form of materialization takes a great deal of energy, and is only performed by a very experience medium under well protected conditions.

It was during a materialization of this type being performed by Helen Duncan, the Police burst in to arrest her. The shock of the arrest caused her physical harm, from which she never fully recovered.

Chapter 25

Clairvoyance, Clairaudience and Clairsentience

Clairvoyance is a form of Spirit communication that we can receive as pictorial information, into our imagination. I find that this information is usually for someone else, but can also be for us. I also consider words that we hear in one's mind as clairvoyance.

Clairaudience, is the term given to messages that are received as an apparent physical sound, either voice or unusual noise. This form of communication I have only experienced on a very few occasions, and it is always a surprise when it occurs.

Clairsentience refers to physical sensations that we experience for which we have no apparent logical explanation. This again is something that I have rarely experienced.

Chapter 26

Clairvoyance

The following is an outline of my development as a Clairvoyant Medium.

The first example that I recognised as a clairvoyant message from someone unknown to me, occurred when attending a cam and tool design course for single spindle screw machines at Browne & Sharpe in Plymouth, U.K.

The hotel at which I was lodged, was a regular spot where people from industry stayed, one chap in particular that was there at the same time as myself, put on a slide show of a visit that he had made to Norway.

He showed slides of a visit to the home of the composer Grieg. The area in which his slides were taken was beautiful, so I mentioned to him that I wish that I would be able to visit such a place. His reply was, "You will one day."

His prediction was quite correct, as living in Canada we see such scenery every day.

I saw this gentleman the following morning and I asked what he did for a living, he said, "I am a plant manager". I replied that is what I hoped to be, his reply this time was, "You will be". I was to eventually hold down such a position at three companies in Canada.

Some 15 years after this event, Barbs made a visit back to England and on this trip she was introduced by my sister in law to a Tarot card reader, Mrs. June Beater.

Barbs was given a reading by June, at the end of the reading, Barbs considered that a good deal of the reading applied to myself.

Her reading proved over time to be right on. Some of her predictions of expected possibilities were that I would undergo an operation on my back, and that I had the best lawyer representing me in regard to the accident that had caused the problem, and also I would eventually be in business for myself.

Knowing nothing at the time of Spiritualism, I thought that the process was fortune telling and that only a few certain special people were able to do this.

Over the next few years of contact with June which included a face to face reading, I gradually learnt more and thought to myself that I would like to be able to bring messages through for others one day.

The results of this wish began to take form in 1995, when our son Keith was terminally ill, due to AIDS related problems. At this time a friend, Roger Leigh of Peterborough, Ontario, suggested that it might be of great help to attend a Spiritualist Church that he was going to, Springdale at 30 Merritt Road, near St. Clair & O'Conner in Toronto.

This church was unlike anything that I had ever known; it was really quite odd as one felt that we had entered a family gathering. I have since realized that one entered for the first time as a stranger but left this church as a friend.

Upon entering this and similar spiritualist churches, we are protected from negative energies, but it is always best to ask for protection when entering an unfamiliar church.

This was the place where my spiritual journey really got going. I went to several Sunday services and on my first visit I was given a message by Rev. Murphy. The message was right on, regarding an aggravating legal problem I had at the time. She told me that I was to answer only the questions that would be put to me and to keep a low profile, then the problem would just fade away. Following the instructions given, the end result was exactly as she suggested.

I met Rev. Bauld one Sunday and she informed me that I would become a Spiritual Healer, which did in time happen.

These messages certainly blew me away, and I became convinced that Springdale Church would be the place that I should go to understand and to learn more about spiritualism.

I then started to attend the open learning circle on Thursday nights at Roger's suggestion. I also read a number of books on how to develop one's psychic abilities, this together with a meditation tape from Rev. Bauld that taught me how to meditate to attune, the opening key for psychic development.

Time was required for practice until with each meditation a wonderful array of moving and changing colours appeared within my closed eye perception.

Everyone, on Thursday nights that sit in circle are asked if they have received any messages to give and as there are usually a number of good mediums sitting in circle, the messages begin to flow. Those who sit in this circle are at different levels of development as everyone progresses at a different rate but all are encouraged to bring forward messages

.

This work can only be at the best level, if everyone understands that it has to be undertaken without ego. Another important requirement for students at Springdale is that no questions or negative messages are allowed, the messages to come straight from Spirit. We give only what we receive. Other mediums ask questions during their clairvoyance, but this leaves them wide open to skeptism.

Please note that all the steps described here, took some time to properly master and it is imperative, that progress is monitored by a very good teacher such as Rev. Bauld.

What I did at first to bring in messages, was to look at someone, and then visualize them on my mind. During these visualizations a scenario would build up around them. These visualizations would then become the basis of messages that I would give in circle. I would also stack a number of messages, to give during the circle.

One of the typical messages that I gave during this period for a lady was, that I could see a building with pointed topped windows and it was raining out side. The building also had a very old wagon beamed roof, but it was not a church. The rain and roof indicated to me that this was in England. I also gave her the name that I think was Maud.

After the service, the lady approached me and told me that they were expecting a visitor from England, whose name I had mentioned. She also noted that this visitor worked as a Librarian in building such as I had described.

Occasional confirmations like this are important, as they help students to be more confident in the messages received from Spirit.

I continued to use this form for messages for quite sometime, until Rev. Bauld suggested that I should start to give verbal messages. Well, I must admit, I was very comfortable with the visual descriptions that I was getting at the time but Rev. must have known that it was time for me to move on.

It was with some trepidation that I began to give messages in word form, after a short time, the messages began to flow quite well. However I was still stacking them.

So the next challenge from Rev. Bauld was for me to give instant messages without stacking. This was a real challenge, but since I had completed a healing course and had started to heal sitters before the circle was held, I had no option but to give instant messages, especially if I was the first to be asked to give messages for the circle.

Typical of the type of messages that I gave and still give in this manner, was one that I gave to a Scottish lady. I told her that I had a gentleman with me and he had said “och, she’s a bonnie wee lassy”. Well, her reaction was emotional, she burst into tears. This, of course took me somewhat aback, until she explained that she had been waiting for this message for a very long time, as it came from her late father in law, for whom she had a great deal of affection. As he always used to say, “och, she’s a bonnie wee lassy”.

I received quite a few messages myself whilst sitting in circle. A number of messages have come and still come through from Keith, some came through a lady in the circle, who was from South America. But one day she came to me and said that she had been informed that she could not get any more through her self from Keith, as he had been working hard in spirit and had advanced to a higher level, to high for her to receive his messages.

She has since gone into spirit and I hope that she and Keith have met.

Another message that I received was through a very good medium, Rev. Vera Molinaro was that she had someone called Jack come through, and he said that I was to stop worrying as my demise was still some time away.

Jack was my cousin who was a year older than I and had just passed on during an operation for stomach cancer. We used to chum around when we were teenagers. So his death had upset me as his age was so close to mine.

Mother has come through quite a number of times, particularly when my brother and I were in conflict, as mentioned earlier.

During this time I had a message from a clairvoyant in the Orillia Church. She saw that I was surrounded with the colour pink, the colour pink meaning love. She also noted something strange, saying that I was also surrounded by flowers. I asked, "What kind of flowers?" the flowers were lilies. Mum's name is Lily.

A couple of weeks later I had a message from a clairvoyant from Oshawa, and she amazingly brought forward the exact same message.

Also as had been predicted my brother would sue us and then give up his case against Barbs and myself.

I also asked mum, a number of times, questioning her actions that caused the conflict with my brother. The next week I received a reply through Re. Bauld, and I was told in no uncertain terms that she knew exactly what she was doing and not to question her motivations again. That put me in my place!

After a number of years of progress, I was asked to join Rev Bauld's advanced circle of six, I was very happy to do this. The circle was held on Wednesday evenings.

Usually, after joining this circle, when I had asked questions of Keith and mother, most of the time I would receive a reply at the next circle.

I have also over the years received other significant messages from Rev. Bauld.

One message was given on a Wednesday at class, that I received from Rev. Bauld, was that I would feel pain in my groin, but not worry as it would not be very serious.

Well I thought at the time, as I was feeling okay, what a lot of old cobblers, but Rev. Bauld's messages were usually right on. On the following Saturday morning, I began to get a very uncomfortable feeling in my lower regions.

I was due that day to go down to Lindsay (Ontario) and then on to Peterborough. Fortunately Barbs said that she would like to go with me, I said okay as the uncomfortable feeling was becoming pain.

Upon arriving in Lindsay, Barbs suggested going into Zellers for lunch, by then the pain was really getting bad, and Barbs said to me, "you look terrible," and knowing that I had not been feeling too good she asked if I wanted to go to the hospital. My reply was"yes". So off we went to the hospital a few hundred yards down the road. A Doctor diagnosed that I had a hernia. I was eventually taken up to the x-ray department and then was prepared for emergency surgery that afternoon.

Quite recently, at a Thursday night circle, a lady that I had seen only a few times, gave me a message stating that mum was standing behind me holding a large yellow flower and coming through with a great deal of love. Again I asked what was the type of flower was mum holding, she replied a Lily!

At another circle, Rev. Bauld gave me a message about someone who had gone into spirit. She stated that this person had come through to thank me for the great help that I was to him at our son's funeral. Rev. Bauld had not attended Keith's funeral, so that she had no pre-knowledge of this event.

As it happened, at the end of the funeral service, one of Keith's closest friends, who was at the time suffering from AID's, broke down saying how lucky Keith was at having parents that had not rejected him because of his life style.

The rejection he had caused him to believe that nobody loved him. I told him that if he took a good look around he would realize that this was not true, as whatever the circumstances, he would find many people both here and the next existence loved him much more than he realized.

It was in 1999, that I received accreditation for Clairvoyance and Lecturing.

I now also do rostrum work in the services and all medium's nights at several Spiritualist Churches.

It must be stressed that my progress to this stage has taken some years, as caution is the watchword, so that advancement is best achieved upon a solid foundation of self control, with the help of a truly gifted teacher.

It should be noted again that at Springdale Church, we are required to give messages without asking questions.

Although we are required not give negative messages, however we are able to give messages of caution, or warnings of possible mishaps and possible poor health conditions requiring attention. The messages that we give are only of possibilities, as events can be changed, by taking avoiding action or seeking medical advice. The recipients of messages are always free to reject them.

Chapter 27

Trance

My first experience with trance was uncontrolled, not realizing that during one of my meditations I had slipped into one, while alone in a quiet isolated room.

When in this trance condition, Keith came through, as through in a clairvoyant dream. He was laughing and kept talking about grandma's black stove but when I tried to come back to this reality, I found that at first I could not, of course I did eventually but with quite a struggle.

My next request was for Spirit not to let this happen again and it has not.

On other occasions when in a trance, I could see groups of people coming into my office, talking quietly so that I could not hear them properly. These would usually end when I heard the door to the room being opened and at this stage I would come back to this reality and find that no one was there.

My further trance work since this experience has only been undertaken within a protected circle environment.

Within our circle, we have visited our guides, our crystal room, been through the veil, received significant messages for the world, and taken part in astral travelling.

Chapter 28

The Great Concordance

In November 2003 what is known as the great concordance occurred, this was an alignment of the planets arranged as the points of the Star of David and coincidentally at the same as time the eclipse of the moon.

At the time of this event, Spiritualists all around the world got together and sat in circle, meditating for world healing.

It was predicted during this event, a split in the time space continuum would be witnessed.

As the eclipse was taking place, our daughter Susan and her husband, who live in Northern Michigan, were outside their house watching the eclipse.

When the eclipse was full, it appeared as though people were looking through the moon at them. After a short time our son Keith was seen to looking through and was saying something that they could not hear. At this point Susan remarked to Keith that she could not believe her eyes, and did not really think that it was him looking through, suggesting to Keith that he would really have to do something for them to know what they were seeing was actually happening.

As a result of her request, the moon then appeared to move around all over the sky. As can be imagined, this really floored Susan and her husband, but it sure was the proof that they had asked for.

To date, I have not seen any other reports of such strange events. This is one experience that to me, confirms that there was a disruption of our reality.

If anyone has experienced something unusual at that time, would they please forward information regarding the event.

Chapter 29

Negative Entities

As explained earlier, Spirit communication, should only be carried out only when proper protection has been established, (i.e. being sure that is asked for)

Before I started to attend Springdale Church in 1995, I had a most unusual experience, as one night I had a very vivid dream. In this dream, of what I considered at the time to be two devils came running towards me.

This really scared me to no end. The first thought that came into my head was that I was to show no fear. This I did, although quaking inside. I then told these entities to buzz off in no uncertain terms.

Upon this request the entities stopped, looked at each other and meekly turned around and much to my relief, went away.

I have since found out, that the approaching characters were from a lower level of existence, known as lower order entities, or creatures from the lower fourth dimension.

These entities can very easily enter thorough the use of ouija boards, as the use of these boards can bypass the protection of the gatekeepers that we all have, and cause us very unpleasant negative problems, up to and including possession. (As mentioned earlier).

Rev. Bauld, and many other mediums and authors of spiritual works, have warned of lower order entities coming through with negative energy, with the use of these boards. So be aware!

The last experience I had occurred after visiting a spiritualist church in Hartford Connecticut, the home of Yale University, in which is the Skull and Bones club. This was the Church of The Infinite Spirit held, as I have mentioned before, in of all places, in a Masonic Hall.

I noticed when entering an illuminated sign, up on the wall, based on an inverted pentagram, a Satanic symbol. I immediately asked for the white light of protection, to prevent any negative energy in the building from having an unpleasant effect on me.

A few nights after returning home from this visit, I had a strange experience, whilst I was awake in bed and I felt a black hole open underneath me with clawed hands trying to pull me into the hole, (lower order entities?). My reaction was, with my knees knocking, to say," okay you guys you can knock that off and go back to were came from!" and away they went.

Control again, very important. It has since been suggested that these episodes were a test of my resolve not to be in league with the Devil.

The understanding that we should all have, is that we must be in control of our own lives. This is very important, as shown from the above examples. We all do have the power to deflect negative entities. There are of course those that welcome these entities into their lives, for personal gain, eventually to regret it.

Chapter 30

Psychometry

This is a process, once outlawed in England, where psychics are able to pick up vibrations of energies by feeling objects and are then able to give some history, of people connected in the past with that object. The reason that it was outlawed was that some unscrupulous so called mediums were making switches with the items that they were given for this practice.

I have found that this process does not work for me but it does work for other mediums.

Great examples of work of this kind, has been shown on the Bravo channel here in Canada in 2005. The title of this program is: "The Antiques Ghost Show".

Chapter 31

Confirmation of Spiritual Presence

Mediums will sometimes be given confirmation of the validity of the messages that the give, either from the recipient, but also directly from Spirit. Some examples of these confirmations are noted below.

Edison's birth place, in Milan Ohio, is now a museum. At this museum over the years their have been a number of reports of strange events, being confirmation of a spiritual presence, i.e. goose bumps with chills or clairaudience. It is therefore possible that Edison is trying to make his spirit energy felt.

Most mediums very often feel this type of energy as described above, when giving significant messages.

I have also experienced this sensation on other occasions. Once, when on a visit to the Imperial War Museum in London I noticed a case on a wall, and I saw that it contained a letter. When looking at the letter I felt a very strong spiritual presence around me causing the hair in the back of my neck to stand up. This letter was brought back from Germany in 1938 by Neville Chamberlain and had been signed by Hitler and himself. The comment that was given by Chamberlain at the time about this letter, was, that he believed that it was peace in our time.

I was born in 1938, and was given the middle name of Neville.

Another occasion happened when I was checking a nursing home for mother, because as soon as I walked into the place, chills gave me the confirmation that this was the best home for her to end her days. This was confirmed a few month's later when mum stated, that as nursing homes go that this was the best one for her to be in.

I also had a very strong feeling of spiritual presence, when I stood on the bridge of the aircraft carrier, the USS Lexington on a visit to Corpus Christi, Texas. The residual energy was very strong; indicating the very powerful emotions of the men who were in command of this ship, during the Second World War in the Pacific. It was very necessary to tell the energies how grateful that I was, as we all should be, for their efforts in that conflict.

Chapter 32

Quantum Physics

The theories of this branch of science have shaken the foundations of materialist and religious dogmas. The theories support in many ways the validity of what Spiritualists have been demonstrating for a long time. I expect the truth to be revealed more and more as time goes on.

Materialists, sceptics and fearful Christians claim that what has been described above cannot be possible but having experienced those events, I do not have to believe that anything is impossible, as Spirit communication has been demonstrated to me. These events indicate that the apparent reality of the Earth plain, is not true reality, but an illusion created by our perception of the vibrating energy that is us and the apparent universe around us.

The phenomenon of quantum physics has shown that parallel universes can indeed exist and explains the how and why of psychic events.

The book by Michael Talbot "The Holographic Universe" is an explanation of our perception of reality, as being an interpretation of holographic vibrations, based on quantum physics. The book also explains that quantum physics shows life energy does not cease to exist upon physical death.

Michael Talbot's book is well worth reading. It is published by Harper Perennial, I S B N #0-06-092258-3.

There is also a movie that explores the subject that certainly opens up minds. This is called, "What The (Bleep) Do We Know?

Chapter 33

Rescues

There is a process known as a rescue for spirits that are caught in limbo between the Earth Plain and the next existence. This is sometimes due to their not knowing that their bodies have died and therefore do not realize that they should try to travel up to the light. Or maybe they want to wait for their resurrection?

The process for rescue is not easy and should only be attempted by experienced mediums, so I shall not elaborate further.

Chapter 34

Group Consciousness

Group consciousness (a group asking Spirit for the same thing) is one of the most powerful ways of raising energy for change, with the human spirit.

Everyone in this world needs to know that this capability is the key that will truly improve the world.

It has often been said that great minds think alike, through which great things can be achieved. Unfortunately, the knowledge of the truth behind this energy has been withheld from the general population of the world for many centuries.

It is a fact that religious political and corporate organizations have actively, and some still actively control large sectors of the world population, by making people believe that their versions of reality is the truth in order to support there agenda.

Indeed this is the root cause of the conflicts from the past up to the present day that have plagued the world. Everyone needs to know that if we use our combined group consciousness, it can heal the world of all the woes that plague us all here. I am expecting one day soon, that this will indeed happen.

Also, those who are seeking control for their own selfish greedy reasons will be continue to be revealed, as some are presently being revealed. This will come about as more and more people are able to see what is really going on in the halls of power and will change things with group consciousness.

It is therefore absolutely essential that the knowledge, regarding the hidden capabilities of all of us is known, and then it will be put to good use.

There have been those in the past that have used, either positive, or negative spirit energies or entities, to achieve their aims. There follows some examples of this form of energy use.

Hitler was a man who is believed to have harnessed the power of lower order entities, (some people would call it selling his soul to the Devil), and so was able to command the group consciousness of the German people. He did this by boldly negating the vengeful mistakes made by the allies after World War 1. This made him emerge as a strong and valiant leader who could resolve all of their problems and so appearing to be their saviour.

To many in Germany at the time he appeared to be a genius, so that he was able to continue with his evil plan to create a New Order in Europe. He eventually failed after causing a great deal of death and destruction in the world. However, when someone such as he makes a pact with the Devil, they will eventually have the rug pulled out from under them.

We should all be aware that apparent genius can be close madness.

We were fortunate that Britain, that when we stood alone, to have a great leader come forward, this was Winston Churchill. He was able to pull the group conscience of the British people together, so that a determined resistance and defiance was bolstered against Hitler.

He did not varnish the truth regarding the difficulties that Britain faced, this made everyone even more determined to resist Hitler. Winston Churchill has acknowledged that he felt sure that he had protection from a spiritual realm, as he remarked that on a number of occasions during the war, that he had some close calls, escaping death by the smallest of margins.

We were also very fortunate that at the same time in Britain's darkest hour, there was another; a spiritualist with an unshakable purpose to defend us to the last. This was Air Chief Marshal, Sir Hugh Dowding, who was able to husband our fighter aircraft resources, that, together with a co-ordinating in depth Radar defence system, which was to help defeat the German Air Force in the Battle of Britain.

I have read one of Lord Dowding's books that I had found recently in the library of Springdale Church. This was a surprise, as this book was about his experiences as a Spiritualist. It is therefore reasonable to assume, that Lord Dowding received inspired help during the dark days of 1940.

It is certainly true that the Christian religion has had a total and uncompromising effect upon the group consciousness of most Europeans and others for many centuries, using the fear of Hell to keep people in line. This condition is certainly changing.

There are still many people in the western world that are trapped in the Christian group mind set, even in the various factions that the church of Rome broke up into. These groups hang onto their mind set through the belief in the Saviour God. This gives them the thought that no matter what they do they will always have their sins forgiven.

Many people over the centuries have been slaughtered in the name of the Christian Church. Those who are presently in charge of the western world, appear on the surface to uphold fundamental Christian beliefs, so that they can force others, by all and any possible means, into there own realm of group consciousness, for their own increase in power, (The New World Order?) But we can see in through the news media that not everyone wants to be taken over.

It is the same reason for the growth of the European empires. History has taught us that no government can never overthrow another country and install its own system of control and beliefs forever, if most of the population of that country does not wish this to happen.

These takeovers have unfortunately created the backlash from some Muslim and other groups, so causing the great problems that we have today. They are of course convinced as individual groups, of the validity of their beliefs, so that we have sparks flying.

Is a situation being created to make the Muslims, and any one else who does not agree with the western idea of freedom and how the world should be, look bad? I hope that this is not true.

It is a task of Spiritualists, to endeavour to help change the group consciences of those in power, and those that believe them to be right, by showing them how to think outside the box of materialism, greed or religion that they are in, and to help them understand the true nature of the universe. This could be an uphill task, as most in power, have a vested interest in maintaining their status quo.

It has been proposed that it will take some world shattering event such as another world war, or a world wide disaster to make those in charge, if they survive, understand that a change in their thinking and attitude to their fellow humans must occur. Current world events indicate that disaster could be a real possibility.

We must all ask or even demand from Spirit that those who seek power and control at the expense of others, should be shown how it is more destructive for them, than for those they are seeking to control and that unconditional love is only the true power of the universe.

We have to ask Spirit, for help in precipitating change without disaster. These requests are ongoing now as at the time of the great concordance, in November 2003.

Remember if we do not ask we will not get the help for ourselves or world change!

Chapter 35

Conclusions

It must be noted again, that we all are psychic some are already or were skilled psychics at birth, which in many cases has been suppressed, by those around us. Luckily there have been those that have been able to overcome this suppression, and have helped others in their psychic development.

There have been very many, with open minds that have become dissatisfied with conventional religion because of its hypocrisy, that feel that there is a higher power, and have also developed their psychic ability, after realizing the fundamental common sense of Spiritualism

The previous examples show that one does not have to believe in anything, as we are told to believe by proponents if conventional religions. The simple fact is that as one develops spiritually, the case for the truth of the universe is demonstrated time and time again.

To those who wish to be closed minded and want to stick to what they are told to believe, such as the saviour god, and that any communication with those that have gone before us is the work of the Devil, I suggest that they stay in their boxed in comfort zone. They will find that once they are through the veil that the truth of the universe will be all too obvious to them.

The story of my progress seems to make spiritualism appear deceptively simple, but it can be deduced that great care and skilled help was required for me to understand what I have learnt up until now. I also know that there is a great deal more yet to understand.

It is important that the motivation that all spiritualists should have is to heal firstly them selves, then to help heal others and the world with unconditional love for all in the universe. Also that we have to continue to help those who have yet to understand the truth of Spiritualism, and to help them understand that life and learning never ends. Real truth can never be disputed. The search for it must continue.

The truly greatest challenge that Spiritualist's have is to find a way, with the help of spirit, to divert those, who through the multinational corporations, are trying to create the new world order, with the manipulation of governments, secret societies and religions, so as to try and control all of us through covert or overt means. Their prime purpose, it seems to be me, is to subjugate us with fear and in extreme cases using trumped up reasons for starting wars.

There is no doubt in my mind that the people behind these organizations that are seeking total control are allied to lower order entities, from which they gain their strength. This, they do not realize, puts them into a position from which they must eventually fall, possibly with dire consequences for the rest of us. Each of us must continue to do what we can to help others and to help heal the world, as the old woman said, every little bit helps!

I recently received a message, that soon we shall be hearing "Oh! How the mighty have fallen". Which means at last maybe, that the meek shall inherit the earth, so that those of us who are able to become truly spiritual will eventually be able to change the world into a much better place?
Remember everyone is psychic!

Thanks, June and Paul

Web Site:- www.geocities.com/terencetompkins

www.ingramcontent.com/pod-product-compliance
Ingram Content Group UK Ltd.
Pitfield, Milton Keynes, MK11 3LW, UK
UKHW040559210726
13854UKWH00008B/1497